Hijacked

Identity

By Sandy Goldmintz

Copyright Page

Kindle Direct Publishing

Cover Picture © Kevin Carden/Adobe Stock

Chapters Index

Introduction

*F*rom the creation of mankind, since satan was cast down from Heaven, bitter envy and hostile jealousy has fueled a fiery spew of venom from him in his murderous attack on God's beloved ones. Israel, most precious to God is a main target, we see throughout the Old Testament from The Beginning with Adam and Eve, Cain and Abel, Moses, the life of Joseph, and Hadassah who became Queen Esther, and David who was overlooked in his own father's eyes and so many of God's chosen vessels leading to when Jesus walked the earth and following His Glorious Resurrection to Saul being radically redeemed into The Apostle Paul who wrote 2/3 of The New Testament.

The list goes on and on, but always the schemes and plots of satan to lie and deceive in his attempts to stop the purpose and destiny God has for each one of us before even the very foundation of the Earth! No new trick, no new game ... a jealous vile murdering thief who is attempting to rob The Living God and take the people God so loves.

This book is soaked in tears, the oil from the crushing and the Anointing of our Holy and Beautiful Father to reach the deepest places of your heart and soul.

Opening Prayer

*M*y prayer is that you would feel the tangible

Love as a healing oil flowing through you, and hear and see His Heart for you! Our Father is a Loving Father and a Mighty Man of War and will move Heaven and Earth to rescue you! What a Loving, Redeeming, Merciful God and Father we have!

Amen.

Dedication

I dedicate this book to my Beloved Father

God, Lord Jesus my Holy Bridegroom –
Warrior King and Holy Spirit my Best Friend
and Teacher, Who fought for me with a
relentless pursuit.

I also dedicate this book to my son Austin D.
Glidewell and my grandchildren Joshua David
Glidewell and Sophia Brooke Glidewell, it is
my heart's cry and prayer that you would each
know deeply the riches of your inheritance in
Christ Jesus and would never struggle in
knowing who God created you to be. May my
ceiling always be your floor in Jesus Name!

Special Thanks

𝐓hanks and honor to Pastor's, Author's and Publisher's John and Susan Perry who came alongside me and poured into me selflessly. May the labor of your love produce a glorious harvest overflowing with beautiful fruit in Jesus Name!

Chapter One

My Not So Grand Entrance into This World

I was conceived in 1967 in sin as a ploy and attempt for my mother to make the man she truly loved jealous. My mother suffered rejection, abuse and abandonment by the true love of her life, which is how "I happened", yet I now know that no child is ever an accident... God planned each one of us to make our grand entry into this world even in the worst situations. God sees everything from the beginning to the end and always has a great and glorious plan for our lives. My family as I am only able to trace from my maternal great grandmother who escaped Auschwitz as a Hungarian Jew after many of her siblings were murdered in the concentration camp, is where I see how fear and shame was fired at her, and the ploy began to *hijack identity and inheritance.*

My maternal great grandmother's name was Katie Berger and she came to America and resided in New York, she married a Catholic Italian man named John Branca and buried her past and heritage. This cycle reproduced when my maternal grandmother Florence also married another Italian Catholic man named Anthony Saccone and the skeletons in the closet continued to pile up.

My mother Carol Katherine was stunning, a cross between Elizabeth Taylor and Sophia Loren, with her own personal-unique beauty. She battled with her weight as many of us do, but her fatal attraction to "bad boys" became a major downfall and cycle that spiraled downwards and became a generational cycle passed down to me. My mother's true love was a man named Paul who was an alcoholic and abuser of women and children due to he himself also being abused as a young child. Prior to my conception he trampled my mother's pregnant womb, beating her for getting pregnant. He refused to marry my mother because he had an ex-wife and 3 children as well as being 17 years older.

My beautiful mother went out night clubbing and met my father Rick who was 3 years younger and hiding behind a mask of lies. My father Richard Joel was born a Jewish man, raised up as an Orthodox Jew and was so ashamed that he took up a fake persona as an Italian man until it could no longer be hidden by my conception.

Wow as I look back, God sent me as a wrecking ball to tear down these strongholds and rebuild ancient ruins. I believe many of you were also sent to do the very same thing in your family lineage! Back to my not so grand entrance... when my mother found out she was pregnant with me, my parents decided to "do the right thing" and get married. The gig was now up, and my parents were married by both a Rabbi and Catholic priest! My Italian mobster uncles calling my dad a "Christ killer" at the wedding, it was drama from the start! I realize both my father and stepfather also had their identities hijacked and needed healing of their souls, I also embrace that what the enemy meant for my harm and destruction... God used for His Glory and to make all things beautiful! So, no matter where you "came from" or how you arrived on Planet Earth, rest assured that God desired you, planned you, and created each one of us for such a time as this.

Regardless of the heartache and trials, you are a song in The Father's Heart and were sent forth with Father's Blessing that will carry you through all the days of your life! We all are God's children who are given to our parents who are earthen vessels. Everyone's story is not the same, some had nurturing parents, some were abused in one way or another, some of you did not know one or perhaps both parents, yet God will always be a Father to The Fatherless! One Kingdom truth remains ... you were no mistake!

I often wondered why I was born into such a "messy situation" until The Holy Spirit began a deep work in showing me, who I am and Who's I am and that I was called to encourage others who struggle as well. We all have inside us such riches of His love and a song of victory to share with others and it is all part of The Gospel and how Jesus heals our broken hearts. If I may encourage you prophetically, "Father God says you are not a mess, you were never a mistake, you are not thrown away trash... you are His beloved child, and He is very pleased with you simply because you are His! You do not have to do anything but belong to Him and accept Him as your Father and He is delighted greatly in you, of course you will want to run down the long dusty trails and bring many prodigals home to The Father's love once you kick off those "shoes of shame" and slide your precious feet into "The sandals of Sonship"!

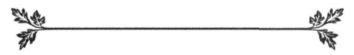

"They will rebuild the ancient ruins, repairing cities destroyed long ago. They will revive them, though they have been deserted for many generations."
Isaiah 61:4 NLT

"He has made everything beautiful in its time. Also, He has put eternity in their hearts, except that no one can find out the work that God does from beginning to end."
Ecclesiastes 3:11 NKJV

Prayer: Father, I Praise You that I am Your Heart's Desire and carry Your very Heavenly DNA. Thank You Lord that You see everything, and You have an amazing plan for my life. I embrace the "new thing" and I leave behind everything that tried to "form me", every label, name and pattern that does not line up with who You created me to be, In Jesus Beautiful Name – Amen.

Activation: Write down on sticky notes all the lies that have tried to define and label you. Invite Holy Spirit to come into this activation... declare out loud; *"In the Name of Jesus, I renounce EVERY lie, EVERY label that has tried to shape my identity and I repent for any agreement I made with any of these lies in Jesus Name- Amen!" (Meditate on Ephesians and create a declaration of truth)*

Chapter Two

Disowned

$\mathcal{M}$y mother had me "Christened" at a Catholic Church and when my father found out, he spit on me and left. Although a baby cannot perceive this, in the realm of The Spirit it's a deep wound and scar. While God is a Father to The Fatherless, my people did not know Him as The Living God, let alone as their Abba Father! My people practiced religion and rituals due to lack of knowledge and understanding; sadly, there was no revelation or intimacy with God.

My mother reconciled with the love of her life Paul sometime later and shockingly enough I have some memories of the abuse, however the trauma that tormented and plagued me for most of my life is finally healed after walking in the effects of deep seeded childhood trauma as well as many years of trauma which led me into a pattern of reacting when confronted as a scared little girl... this is what is called a fragmented mind, BUT... God worked a creative miracle - Hallelujah! Nothing is too hard for God; He can rewire our brains and yank trauma out at the very root from even a cellular level because He is The One Who formed us. Oh, what a wonderful healing God we have!

Paul resented me due to his jealousy towards my own father and his abuse of myself and my mother grew. I profoundly remember a few incidents as a 2-year-old hiding behind her and the belly of my pregnant mother after Paul threw my childhood rocking chair with me in it across the room because I was watching cartoons. I also recall being placed on a sled that was tied to an Alaskan malamute as Paul yelled **"MUSH!"** All I remember is fear as the sled wrapped around a tree and beyond this, I can't recall anything other than I developed a kidney stone and can remember the pain of passing it as a toddler. Trauma can have an impact on our health in many ways. What we experience in the spiritual can manifest in the natural whether positive or negative!

My brother Erik was born in 1970 and not much time afterwards Paul abandoned us, which I'm now so grateful for. We were spared a lifetime of abuse from his violent hand and cruel mouth. I am also now very aware that Paul was abused as a child as well and mixed with alcoholism, rage and anger, he truly needed an encounter with The Father, and I pray he had one before he passed away.

My maternal grandfather Anthony, who I called Papa had a dream to move to Florida, so he and my grandmother began building a house for my mother, my aunt, me and my brother to live in. I was told I was the *"apple of my Papa's eye"* profoundly to me now and very prophetic symbolically! I have some memories of him brushing my hair and being kind to me as a young child. Papa became very ill with pancreatic cancer and passed away before ever making it to Florida and my family moved.

My mother decided to *"change my identity"* due to shame, so that nobody would know my half-brother and I had different fathers. The skeletons were piling up in the closet of my lineage yet as the Prophet called dry bones to life, it would be in *my awakening spiritually that I too prophesied to every dry bone!* I am certain each of us have had "skeletons in our closet" or a "white elephant in the room" that nobody wants to talk about, but Jesus wants to talk with you about these things and give you a brand-new garment from His Family lineage...a Heavenly Garment!

"And He said to me, "Son of man, can these bones live?" So, I answered, "O Lord God, You know." Again, He said to me, "Prophesy to these bones, and say to them, 'O dry bones, hear the word of the Lord! Thus says the Lord God to these bones: "Surely I will cause breath to enter into you, and you shall live."
Ezekiel 37:3-5 NKJV

Prayer: Father, I praise and thank You that You foreknew me before the very foundation of the earth, You sung over me and as my substance swirled around You like a Glory Cloud! You rejoiced and laughed knowing the plans You have for me are wonderful! I decree and declare I am a child of destiny; I will fulfill my purpose to bring You great Glory and Praise, In Jesus Might Name – Amen

Activation: I encourage you to see with The Eyes of The Spirit and The Heart of The Father, the beautiful *"Glory colors"* of your spiritual DNA (your substance) swirling around as The Father delights in you!

Do you feel His warm tender love filling you fresh even now?
Linger in His love a moment... just LINGER!

Chapter Three

Who's That Girl?

I was born Sandra Suzanne Goldmintz and by the time I was 4 years old, I was overweight and thought I was the daughter of Paul because my name had been *illegally* changed by my mother. In the 70's this was so easy to get away with by merely putting corrective tape and typing a new name, then making copy after copy until it looked real!

My story although not as glamorous as Queen Esther runs a similar theme of satan and his schemes to destroy identity. Hadassah's Jewish roots *were hidden* as she entered King Ahasuerus' (King Xerxes) Palace becoming Esther per the prompting of her uncle Mordecai. Yet, God's purpose manifested gloriously! Likewise, in my own personal story... I liken it to a walk through a garden that was filled with weeds and not flourishing until God poured "revelation rain" upon the very roots of my foundation many years later.

My identity of being a Jewish girl was being watered down into a pattern of lies as I entered elementary school a shy, overweight girl who had learned as a baby and toddler what rejection, abandonment and stuffing in the pain was. As the teases and taunts came in "fatty four eyes", "fat – ugly, four eyed girl". I learned to "stuff it" deep inside, however stuffing food in my mouth as a false means of comfort began a cycle which only worsened my self-esteem.

Growing up in my family household consisted of my maternal grandmother, mother, aunt, brother and myself and as dysfunctional as it was, they did the best they could to raise us. There was a lot of name calling such as "you fat slob" and saying "Omar the tent maker would need to be called to make our clothes", yet extravagant Christmas gifts, birthday gifts and family vacations mingled in through it all. I would say a roller coaster of dysfunction!

One traumatic memory that really stayed with me most of my life was when I was 9 and my brother 6, we had a sibling argument, my mother pulled into an orphanage and told us she was going to leave us there. I believed her as she opened the door and told us to get out! As fear, tears and grief grabbed ahold of me it soon ended as she put us back in the car. There were many wonderful memories and lots of bittersweet and painful memories too.

I had severe asthma as a child and allergies as well as a lump developed on my left arm requiring tests, thankfully it was only a "fatty tumor" which later I will tell you how the enemy started his attacks of disfigurement to further destroy my life and identity. These "events" of infirmity are rooted in fear, trauma, abandonment, rejection, abuse, self-hatred, self-loathing, self-rejection and anger. How can a baby, a toddler, a young child truly perceive how to forgive?

My identity was altered and hidden for 11-1/2 years until the day I found my baby book and saw my real last name with a line drawn through it and Paul's last name written in place.

Many of you reading this, were born and given up for adoption into a new family and perhaps do not know your natural parents, but we thank God right now that your parents chose to give you the gift of life as opposed to abortion... I celebrate your life right now! Many of you were molested by a parent or family member, abused, beaten, neglected, yet I encourage you to let Jesus into that memory and allow the Sword of The Spirit (God's Word) be a "Physician's Scalpel" and uproot all the trauma. I bless your life and I thank God for your life and your story that is being rewritten and edited by God. For Only God has the "Heavenly Eraser" to give us brand new identities and heal our hearts and memories!

While this book is <u>not</u> meant solely as a biography of my life, it is a living testimony and God is pouring oil upon the ink you are reading which will shatter the shackles that have attempted to hijack your own identity!

Although my father and my mother have abandoned me,
Yet the Lord will take me up [adopt me as His child]. Psalm 27:10 AMP

But now, O Lord, You are our Father,
We are the clay, and You our potter;
And all of us are the work of Your hand.
Isaiah 64:8 NASB1995

Prayer: Abba, my Father for You truly are The Potter and I am the clay, mold me, fashion me into who You truly designed me to be. Father, right now in Jesus Mighty Name, I am asking you to reach deep into my heart and uproot every root of trauma, abandonment, abuse and rejection and pour Your Love as a healing oil. Even right now my Father would You baptize me fresh in Your Perfect Love? I know You delight in me and have placed a royal ring upon my finger, a robe of righteousness around my shoulders and "shoes of Sonship" upon my feet. I take a step forward right now, kicking off the dust receiving Your beautiful gift of adoption and Your exquisite love. I decree and declare: *"I am royalty; I am who You say I am. I was born with a purpose and divine destiny and from this moment forward will keep my eyes forward on eternity and the amazing - glorious plans You have for me in Jesus Beautiful and Holy Name – Amen!"*

Activation: Allow yourself to be swept away into the image of how the prodigal ran towards Father, *see Him* running passionately towards you, and feel Him placing that royal ring upon your finger and that robe around your shoulders. Hear His voice of love declaring you are His and how He celebrates you!

Isn't His Love sweet, deep and powerful? Do you feel the healing virtue of His love going deep-deep-deep into every fiber of your being? We praise You Father!

Chapter Four

Am I Adopted?

Torment flooded the very depths of my soul as I gazed at the baby book and ran to my mother for answers. My mother told me her version of the story and when I asked where my Father was she stated, *"I don't know, he changed all his information and we can't locate him for child support."* An 11 1/2-year-old girl would believe her mother and now the spirit of rejection took further root as a tsunami of emotions ran wild.

Growing up my half-brothers' grandparents had followed my mother to Florida, during those years I had a close bond with whom I thought was my grandmother, so I ran over to her house which was only a half block away.

Teary eyed I said *"Grandma, I know you're not my real grandmother, but I love you the same and you will always be my grandma! "*

Her response was like a sword into my heart as she went into a spiel about why she had never taken me or my brother to Switzerland replying, *"After all, Sandy you are not my real granddaughter!"*

That dart went in deeply with the venom of illegitimate poison laced in rejection to mingle with all the other unhealed soul wounds and further shatter a young child's heart so that an expectation of rejection, abandonment, abuse and trauma was a self-taught and toxic coping skill. When you are always waiting for the other "shoe to drop" bracing yourself for more hurt, how can healing ever flow? *Without a knowledge and revelation of God*, The Father loving us with an everlasting love, a Father who unrelentingly pursues and fights for us... otherwise we will continue to walk in an *"Orphan Spirit with open – bleeding soul wounds!"*

Thankfully and humbly, I can say His Love is all the healing we need and once that kiss of revelation comes... healing flows like an unrestrained river manifesting gloriously. Most of the time this is a process when there are "Daddy wounds" present and even "Mommy wounds". *(The loving, protective side of Men comes from Papa God and beautiful nurturing side that women have is part of Gods nature)*

I walked in an orphan spirit almost my entire life up until my encounter with The Lord, and during this encounter God revealed He was my true Father and my parents were but earthen vessels. This tender encounter transformed my life and shifted my thinking. It was indeed a process due to all the years walking in this orphan spirit, yet The Father ALWAYS comes RUNNING!

There is not a person alive who has not experienced some form of trauma or rejection no matter the depth of the wound. You can come from a great- functional family with a loving, protective father and nurturing mother, yet still have a disconnect that could be caused from something generational in the past, or by an experience you may have had with another individual. When we reflect on Joseph's life there was so much jealousy amongst his siblings, that even his parents did not accept his prophetic dreams. It was while Joseph endured a long – hard road... he came forth as gold to restore and sustain his family. God always wins and always has The Master Plan! He holds the Blueprints of your life in His Hand and He has called you by name... you are His!

If you feel like you have messed up your life too badly for repair, let me encourage you that while God made us powerful in Him... we are not that powerful enough to stop the amazing plans God has for us. Never – ever give up on yourself...God doesn't!

My heart is branded by God to *release strength, healing and love and that an impartation of "the warrior inside you" to awaken and rise as the beloved and accepted child of God that you are!*

"The entire universe is standing on tiptoe, yearning to see the unveiling of God's glorious sons and daughters!"
Romans 8:19 TPT

"and I will be a father to you, and you shall be sons and daughters to me, says the Lord Almighty."
2 Corinthians 6:18

Prayer: Oh Lord, my wonderful and Holy Father... You have brought me out of darkness into Your Glorious Light. You have kissed my eyes with Revelation Light and Your very hand has reached in deep to remove the lies, the scars and pain, even as far back as when I was in my mother's womb. You have blessed my birth and proclaimed a Father's blessing over me, and I know my birthright is restored unto You. You oh Lord signed my spiritual birth certificate and I rejoice greatly in being hand picked by You the Most High God- my Father. I am Yours and You are mine – Hallelujah!

Activation: In your Bible or journal or even on the computer, create a special "Birth Certificate" and sign it by Your Holy Father Yahweh!

Declare with me: *"I was born of The Most Royal Lineage; My Father is God Almighty and His very finger signed my spiritual birth certificate! I am thankful for my parents who God chose as vessels to bring me forth and I honor my mother and father. No matter where I have come from, I have a rich inheritance and an eternal future!"*

Chapter Five

Looking for Acceptance

*W*hen you believe the implanted lies of the enemy, they become a foreign part of your entire being, however your spirit man rejects this, and your physical body will wage war against itself. Think of how a person's body can reject breast implants, or any implant not designed by The Master Artist, Father God. You, beloved are His Masterpiece, created for His Glory!

This is how many autoimmune diseases and sicknesses take root, self-loathing and self-hatred are contrary to God's Heart and conflicts with the treasured spirit you are, that He foreknew and sings over; the very essence of your being that He so dearly loves and created with purpose and destiny. I can remember just wanting to belong and be loved. I was not aware I was already loved with an everlasting love or that I had a Father who would stop at absolutely nothing to reveal Himself to me and kick down and destroy by The Fire of His Zeal and Love every barrier, every lie, and every wall.

In my disillusionment, rebellion and wandering is how I was molested at the young – tender age of 12 and that led to a destructive pattern years down the road of promiscuity. That same year, my mother became a correctional officer; we did not see her very much as she worked the night shift a lot. She decided to move out and took my brother and me to a hotel and I remember us staying there alone while she worked overnight. My grandmother and aunt somehow got involved and there was a dispute between them and my mother. My mother left us with my grandmother and aunt and there was talk of them adopting us. I was angry and continued my rebellious cycle and learned quite young to be a people pleaser which seemed to never truly work.

My mother "disappeared" shortly after for 3 months and my grandmother and I went to her apartment, to find it vacant with no clue of where she went. On my thirteenth birthday my mother returned and promised to never leave us again. I recall swearing never to do the things she did, however I did indeed do similar things later down the road. "Inner vows" always lead us to a place of attracting what we vow never to do, unless we renounce it.

Steeped in self-loathing and anger my teenage years were filled with boyfriends, partying and sleeping around. I was looking for someone to love and accept me, but I did not love or accept myself. I spent years of toxic repetitive cycles. My self-confidence was so low, and I always felt a feeling of unworthiness, or not good enough. I was entrenched in shame, and I would lose weight by starvation then gain it all back which replayed this pattern like a stuck record! I was always trying to fit in and I can remember season upon season of being last picked for the sports we played in school.

At age 17, a lump in my left leg appeared and I was at a doctor appointment with my grandmother when he looked at me and said, "What happened, did your boyfriend kick you in the leg?" I shrugged this off not knowing I was developing a disfiguring affliction called primary lymphedema which would grow and disfigure my legs mostly. Remember the "fatty tumor" as a young child? I believe this was the start of this vicious cycle. As I got older, I assumed I just had "big legs "and my way of coping was more self-destructive behavior and my inward hate towards myself grew deeper taking root in the soil of all the pain and turmoil within me. Looking for love in all the wrong places is the road that led me to tolerate years of abuse, physically, emotionally, verbally and later even spiritually!

Self-medicating with food, drinking, drugs, pornography, alternative lifestyles later in my adult life, opened the doors and windows to the demonic realm to enter and torment me as well as years later manifesting into sickness and disease. Even radical gastric bypass surgery at age 37, which does not heal spiritual and emotional issues.

Truly without an encounter with The Lover of our souls either through His Word, revelation or supernaturally, we will often consider ourselves "damaged goods" or "hopelessly defective" which is the biggest lie because we are made in God's very image and likeness. We are The Apple of His eye. He sees everything and He sees us whole. When we finally embrace this, we will see the spiritual manifest into the physical.

All throughout the Bible we see account after account of how Jesus transformed the most desperate and hopeless situations including disfigurement. Jesus Himself was disfigured so we could be made whole. Can you even wrap your mind around the pain and torment Jesus suffered to pay in full for the punishment we deserved? He was sent to rescue and restore us, and to be our Kinsman Redeemer? Wow, I forever stand in awe... What a Savior, what a Friend, what a Beautiful and Holy King!

But he was wounded because of our crimes,
crushed because of our sins;
the disciplining that makes us whole fell on
him, and by his bruises* we are healed.
Isaiah 53:5 CJB

But Christ proved God's passionate love for us by dying in our place while we were still lost and ungodly!
Romans 5:8 TPT

Prayer: Father, thank You that there is no stain or scar that The Blood of Jesus cannot wash away and heal! Jesus my Holy King, I ask You Lord to embrace Your son or daughter reading this prayer and allow the Fire of Your Love to consume anything that has made them feel unwanted, discarded or dirty. Lord, You redeem us and You redeem the time because You are outside of time! Holy Spirit thank You for making Jesus so tangible and real to the son or daughter reading this prayer right now that they will be embraced in Perfect Love and kissed with grace! Father, I pray against trauma – physically, spiritually, emotionally that right now You would uproot it at a cellular level and all the effects of that trauma, Lord. We know that Your Word is alive and active, sharper than any double-edged sword and penetrates even to the dividing soul and spirit, joints and marrow (Hebrews 4:12); by this we know and believe that this is so easy for You, and we praise and thank You for this miracle in Jesus Matchless and Holy Name – Amen and Amen – Hallelujah!

As you read and meditate on the prayer, no matter your story... God can and will turn it around for His Glory! Your story is a powerful testimony that will unshackle and bring hope and healing to someone else!

Decree: I decree and declare that my past was just a sheet of music in Gods hands. God is writing my song to bring triumphant and glorious praise to His Name. The sad, broken parts of my song are just a bridge to the chorus of victory set to the melody of Perfect Love in Jesus Holy Name – Amen!

Chapter Six

Bandages and Bondages

*E*arlier in chapter 3, I said this was not intended to be a biography so as I bridge into how I met Jesus "Face to face", I will bring us quickly from my youth to the summer of 2012! Buckle up; we are moving at light speed!

In 1989 our lives were turned more upside down when my mother died of lung cancer at the young age of 47 (I was 21.) I was angry at a God I didn't know, and this led me into a self-destructive pattern of drugs, and reckless relationships. I met my son Austin's father in 1991 and married quickly even though he had cheated on me before and during my pregnancy! I was overjoyed to become a mother and embraced being pregnant. My son's father wanted only a boy and I remember feeling so scared that he would reject me and the baby if I was pregnant with a girl. He refused to go to any of my OBGYN appointments with me and the day I learned I was having a boy, I hoped this would change his heart towards me. Sadly, it didn't because I didn't love myself enough and accepted the lies of unlovable, unworthy of love this produced the fruit of toxic relationships.

My son Austin is such a precious gift to me from God and I'm thankful God had His hand on his life since his birth. I stand in awe looking at how God is always there even when we are too blind to recognize Him. So, what do you think happens when you don't know who you really are and worse yet WHO's you are … a daughter or son of The Most High God? Well, the law of attraction begins working negatively as satan becomes the director of an attempt to rob, steal, kill and destroy. Two spiritually unhealthy people attempting to raise an innocent child and although we loved our son, our toxicity towards one another was producing a weedy – thorny garden. I learned quite early on to "put on a happy face "and smile even though inside my heart was breaking. I threw myself into work and my husband and I grew further and further apart.

We purchased our first computer in 1999 and a stronghold began to form when I discovered I could escape my reality when I developed a false online name and identity. As you can probably guess my marriage disintegrated as my husband smoked pot and drank while I dove into "fantasy land" developing a porn addiction on top of it all! We divorced in 2001 and my life was now fueled with more strongholds of porn and sex addiction, anything to numb my reality and escape! I threw myself into work and climbed the corporate ladder yet the void inside me and the turmoil took me to paths of more darkness.

Sadly, my son was affected by this because he spent most of his time with my aunt. I always loved my son dearly with all my heart, he has always been such a blessing and gift from God, yet I had strongholds of addiction that drove me to become careless. I am thankful to this day that God redeemed all the time and my son, and I have such a precious -strong and loving relationship.

Escaping serves as only a "quick fix" and when the "fix" runs out the crash is hard leaving you to seek more and more of a way out of facing yourself, always searching, always seeking, never satisfied. The only "True Escape" is Jesus, The Way, The Truth and The Life! He will never leave you feeling empty and unwanted, He will always affirm you as His most treasured and beloved treasure!

Jesus answered her, if you had only known and had recognized God's gift and Who this is that is saying to you, Give Me a drink, you would have asked Him [instead] and He would have given you living water.
John 4:10 AMPC

"Father, I have manifested who you really are and I have revealed you to the men and women that you gave to me. They were yours, and you gave them to me, and they have fastened your Word firmly to their hearts."
John 17:6 TPT

Prayer: Father, our feet have traveled some roads that You did not intend for us to ever walk down. We are grateful that You apply healing balm to our weary feet and wash our feet with love and kindness. We have a glorious book You wrote for our lives and no time is ever truly wasted once we come face to face with You. Thank You for the dust behind us and the Glory in front of us in Jesus Majestically Holy Name – Amen!

Activation: Invision yourself taking a very overstuffed heavy backpack off your shoulders and some suitcases and duffel bags that are filled with your past mistakes and regrets and laying them at the feet of Jesus. *See* His eyes of Fire, His eyes of Love gazing upon you passionately as He whispers "I am delighted to take them, are you sure you want to give them to Me?" As you give Him your "Yes Lord!" feel the weight lift off your shoulders and *see* the Radiant Beauty of His Love as He says, "My yoke is easy and My burden is light, you were never meant to carry that My Beloved one!"

Rest in His Love and experience "The Beautiful Garment" He has placed upon you, marking you forever in His victorious and treasured child!

44

Chapter Seven

The Highway to Hell But God So Loved!

*I*n my journey to be, loved and belong to someone, I entered alternative lifestyle's dabbling in Wicca as well as allowing myself to be used and abused sexually. I hated it yet the wilder it got, the more accepted I felt because I thought in my striving, if I would be the most outrageous doing close to anything, I would be loved and deemed worthy of love. In this chaos, I placed my parenting responsibilities primarily on my aunt as I mentioned earlier, and irresponsibly went to several states in my seeking love.

When I was so tired of the pain physically, I dove seriously into a career and tried to make up for lost time with my son, yet the damage was done. Now toppling the scales at 368 lbs. I opted for radical gastric bypass surgery, this is when the diagnosis of primary lymphedema was first told to me, yet the reality didn't set in immediately. I excitedly watched weight melt off me however I was not prepared for the loose sagging skin which led me into more self-loathing and shame.

I went to see a plastic surgeon who informed me that he could not touch my legs due to the lymphedema but would remove loose skin from my arms and give me a breast implant surgery and tummy tuck. I had a melt down and left in hysterics telling my fiancé at the time that he can dump me because I would look like a freak! This fiancé was a free mason and womanizer who I thought I was madly in love with, but this relationship was so damaging spiritually as well as emotionally that it would take years to be free of that stronghold.

I allowed more violation in my relationship with him, when he told me "You cannot afford to be picky with your legs", so it was another cycle of me trying to do anything to keep this man who ended up cheating on me and giving me an STD (which since I have been healed of, thank You Jesus for Your love and mercy!)

When I finally got away from him after a cycle of him stalking me at my job and attempting to blackmail me, I met a man on the rebound who told me I was the most beautiful woman and although he didn't seem particularly mentally stable, I embraced the romancing and dived in.

I ended up marrying him only after a few months after partying all night on St. Patrick's Day because he needed health insurance due to a scare that occurred with his heart and a trip to the hospital. This began a 3-month cycle of abuse both physically, sexually and emotionally and even attempting to keep me captive from going to work by cutting up my bras. At this point I had lost a tremendous amount of weight and after he was cruel to my now teenage son, I left him. For a few months, I received death threats however his stalking attempts failed, and I was able to successfully divorce him!

I decided I was talking a break from dating and continued to work on my physical appearance however without the "spiritual make-over" that only comes from a love encounter with Jesus, all we have is something that fades and washes away like make- up!

I began going out dancing, nightclubbing, ladies night and drinking with a friend from high school's older sister who was also divorced. We recklessly drove drunk, had one-night stands and became groupies for a local rock band and although I thought I was living, deep inside I was drowning in an illusion!

I was empty and filled with self-destruction and self-hatred. I had met a man on social media who I had known in Jr. High and High School, and he began flirting with me and following me on social media. A year and a half later I went to meet him and while he seemed to be kind and sweet, he had built the foundation upon lies from the beginning. While he said all the charming, sweet words and made me "feel" pretty and loved, the deception began to unravel, and I found out he was a hard-core alcoholic. I was so very co-dependent at that time in my life that I thought I could fix him! Pretty ironic because I needed to be fixed myself but that is the way of a co-dependent. He had a lovely family, and I deeply loved his mother and sister and still to this day I do!

Shortly after his father passed away in 2011, his drinking binges turned to violence and while he had always been excessively jealous and controlling... it now took on a new spin! The drinking would begin in the morning and end late at night and the violence of shoving and grabbing me, led to him beating me to a raw bloody pulp that almost killed me! This was what should have been my wake-up call and in many ways it was, because I did leave him, bought a home far away and pursued Jesus giving up alcohol and partying forever!

In the summer of 2012 after sustaining a severe head and face trauma from his drunken rage as I was driving and helpless was the wake-up call that I should have answered and let it be a permanent warning! I moved across the state, purchased my home and got before The Lord crying out *"I know and believe You are real, please help me and make Yourself real to me!"* His Presence came in like a flood and my life began to change, I got plugged into a little church and unfortunately one day shortly after his mother showed up at my front door with him and she started begging me, crying for me to please take him back. Desperately she pleaded with me that she had made his father a promise to never allow either of her sons to live with her. I weakened seeing her pain and let him in. You might be thinking "Is this woman crazy, out of her mind?" Yes, in fact I was so damaged that *I had no sense of identity* other than I knew I loved Jesus.

He had stopped drinking and began attending church with me and I thought things would be okay. I learned to forgive him and thought I was putting everything behind us. The things we do for love when we are wounded and do not have the *correct lenses of God's love and identity* of who we are as chosen, and beloved children of God can be detrimental on all levels! Through it all I grew closer and closer to God and developed a deep relationship with The Holy Spirit.

Isn't Jesus so beautiful how He takes us in our worst messes and calls us His own? He is truly The Lover of our souls, The Healer of our hearts and The Restorer of the Breach!

I do not know what cycles and path's you have walked through as no two stories are identical but what I do know is that Jesus is really The Fourth Man in The Fire and has been with us in every situation even when we had no clue, He was our ever-present help in times of trouble!

To console those who mourn in Zion, to give them beauty for ashes, The oil of joy for mourning, The garment of praise for the spirit of heaviness; That they may be called trees of righteousness, The planting of the Lord, that He may be glorified."
Isaiah 61:3 NKJV

Then Jesus stood up again and said to the woman, "Where are your accusers? Didn't even one of them condemn you?"
"No, Lord," she said.
And Jesus said, "Neither do I. Go and sin no more."
John 8:10-11 NLT

Prayer: Lord, as I look back upon my life even the worst, most dark areas, the most horrific and heartbreaking events; I can see that You were there, You kept me because You see the BIG picture for You are The Author and Finisher of my faith. To the one who was thrown away, rejected, abandoned, abused, raped, molested, beaten whether it is physically, spiritually, verbally or emotionally... would You kiss their eyes with Revelation light and love and show them how You see them in The Spirit even right now Lord? For every regret You have a garden of testimonies ready to blossom as You water the seemingly wilted flowers with Your Holy Healing Rain of Love. Father in Jesus Name I ask You to infuse this precious child right now with hope and Your extravagant love so deeply that they will know beyond a shadow of a doubt how deep The Father's Love is for us! I ask this all in the Mighty Name of Jesus – Amen!

Activation: Stand up and take a deep breath as You release the breath, close Your eyes for a moment seeing the garden of Glory in front of you! After opening your eyes declare boldly,

"My trials are now my Testimonies, my heartbreak is now my strength to bring restoration and hope to another. Father, I will keep my eyes fixed on Eternity and this gift You so freely gave me... I shall go freely carrying living water from the well of Your love to other dry and thirsty souls in Jesus Holy Name – Amen!"

Chapter Eight

Awakening First Love

Often in our journey we feel dirty and do not perceive how a Holy God would want to come close to us in our mess and sin, but let us remember how Jesus loves to step into the mess with us and take the broken pieces in His Holy Hand to create a Masterpiece for His Glory!

Look at the story of the woman at the well and see how broken this precious daughter was until Perfect Love stepped into the scene of her mundane life of shame. This daughter was fully restored and became the first female evangelist who forever holds a place in The Lord's heart and in The Bible! (John 4) Let's reflect on the woman caught in the very act of adultery, can you feel her shame, the fear, the hostility that she felt in that very accusing moment in which she thought her life was about to be over?

Jesus lifted her head up and rescued her from being condemned to die; He stepped outside The Law because Love is Stronger and Forever Enduring. He rescued her as He rescues us because God so loves each one of us that He sent Jesus to fulfil The Law yes, but to bring The New Covenant, a more Perfect Covenant to redeem all God's beloved children that He loved and knew before we were even placed upon this earth!

This daughter's destiny was forever sealed and changed by Love... Pure Love that washed all the yuck and filth away so she could shine for The Lord as His treasured daughter and begin again in garments of praise! (John 8) Wow... that is each of us; we all have a past whether it is just a few lines out of the color page of life or a page of scribble scrabble... God gives us a new pallet for His Hand to create a portrait of purpose, testimony and beauty! We can learn from the beautiful testimonies in The Word of all lives transformed in a Heartbeat when Perfect Love encountered their lives!

So, we come as we are to Him for, we cannot make ourselves clean only His Love can do the work. I was broken beyond what in the natural realm would be unable to repair but God stepped into my mess with me and He has never stopped reaching, loving, healing, mending, rescuing and He never will! During my baby Christian days, I simply wanted to know Him, to hear Him and it was almost effortless even in the midst of an abusive controlling marriage I leaned upon Him and learned to worship and praise Him which was my greatest joy and He met me!

In the fall of October 2013, I was given an opportunity to go on a women's retreat, a lady told me I would come face to face with Jesus and as a child I wholeheartedly believed her! A few days prior to going on the retreat, I was walking and interceding for others in my daily prayer walk when suddenly I heard The Lord for the first time audibly asking me "How come you have not asked me to heal your legs?" I stopped abruptly in my walk and answered as a baby Christian would "Lord, it is not that I didn't think You could, I just didn't know You would!"

This very pivotal moment of my life was an infusion of great faith and an invitation to come closer, every fiber of my being vibrated with wonder and hope! Worship was my beginning of entering The Secret Place, truly I did not know in the beginning of my journey with Jesus how to do anything but lift up my hands and sing to Him but He always came and a passion for Him ignited a hunger I never knew!

The week before the retreat my husband went on the men's retreat, however he came home accusing me of cheating on him with a neighbor and I was so hurt by his accusations and cruel words. I was still determined to go and believe for an encounter with Jesus.

On the retreat, I was expecting to come face to face with Jesus, I followed the rules and put my cellphone away during the day and spent time listening to the teachings and meditating, worshipping and learning all about forgiveness. I was so unhappy in my marriage and wanted out of the marriage almost a week after marrying him. The final evening of the retreat, after writing down all the people I needed to forgive I realized I was struggling to forgive myself for having an abortion when I was 17 and for all my other mistakes. As I stepped out on "the water of trusting Jesus," that He really forgave me, I wrote my own name at the bottom of the piece of paper.

We were led into a tent that was dedicated to being a chapel as my turn came, I knelt before a little pool of water and placed my paper into the water, as it dissolved no one laid hands on me but the Power of God came on me as I had never experienced, and every fiber of my being was shaking like an earthquake! I had absolutely no grid for the supernatural and sat down in a chair shaking violently. This kind lady wrapped her arm around me and kept saying "It's okay honey, it's okay", I remember digging my feet into the ground trying to stop this shaking, but it did not stop.

That night I was awakened to what sounded like a shofar and in the morning, I asked if anyone had sounded a shofar and was told no, I also noticed I had lost some of the fluid in my lower legs and my jeans were looser, so I knew God had begun something and others noticed

this also. From that point on, my eyes had been opened and life was not the same as usual anymore, it was a whole new world...
The Supernatural World!
I left the retreat invigorated and excited to follow Jesus no matter where He took me, I was forever changed!

She has been forgiven of all her many sins. This is why she has shown me such extravagant love. But those who assume they have very little to be forgiven will love me very little."
Luke 7:47 TPT

Many of the Samaritans from that town put their trust in Him because of the word of the woman testifying, "He told me everything I ever did!"
John 4:39 TLV

Prayer: Jesus, thank You for coming into my mess, stepping into the scene of my life. You are not afraid to get Your hands dirty for in fact, there is no fear in You because You are Perfect Love in Living Expression!

Father, You sang over me when I was just a dream in Your Heart, a song of love deep in the chambers of Your Holy Heart. Take me back today to my First Love, awaken me from any area where I have fallen asleep or where the cares of this world have weighed me down. I praise You for Your songs of deliverance and love being constantly sung over my life. Let my life be a song that brings You great pleasure and joy my Loving Faithful Father, in Jesus Beautiful Name – Amen and Amen!

Activation: Perhaps you have forgiven and written down names of people who have hurt you before, but I ask you now to partner with Holy Spirit to see if there is anyone, *especially yourself* that you need to forgive. Only in The Strength of Jesus is this possible and it is not based on a "feeling!" If so, why not right now take a piece of paper and write out the name or the names and release that paper into a sink or pool of water this very day. Let the "Water of The Word" wash it away and watch the paper disintegrate and the ink blur until it cannot be read! Just as The Lord blots out our transgressions, this is a prophetic act of following in His Holy Footsteps! As you step out in faith, ask The Lord if there are any barriers, any hindrances or walls that are trying to silence His Love song over you?

Declare with me: *"Father, I know Your voice for I am Your sheep, Your child who You treasure and I ask for a refreshing today of First Love, a new encounter with Your Spirit as my heart desires to love You deeper, richer and to love Your people that You gave ALL for deeply and with Holy Fervor the way You love me Holy Father.*

I decree and declare that I am love because I am made in Your Image and that blessed are my eyes for they see, blessed are my ears for they hear, blessed is my heart for it understands and perceives what The Spirit is saying. I proclaim today is a pivotal point in my life no matter what has happened for You are The God Who parted The Red Sea and nothing is impossible to You Lord. I praise You and give You myself fresh and new this very day and all The Glory and Honor belongs to You Forevermore, Lover of my soul, in Jesus Holy Name – Amen!"

Take this precious moment in time to mediate on His love which is so rich and multi-faceted, spend time worshipping Him and breathing in His Love and Life! Journal any tender words He speaks to you, even a scripture verse He brings fresh revelation of!
This is a Holy moment.

Chapter Nine

The Glory Reverberates Your Story

*W*e see in The Prodigal Son a perfect snapshot of how our Father views us when we turn to Him and run home to His Love and Protection. Jesus revealed this to us purposefully to brand us with a love story upon our hearts of a Holy Father who never gives up on us and always welcomes us back with great joy and open Arms! (Luke 15:11-32)

No matter how deep we are in the mire and pig slop, Jesus is waiting and ready to pull you out and Father is ready to celebrate your return home and fully restore you to His original plan and design. One of the tactics of the enemy is to try to make us think God is mad at us and will reject and punish us but that is a lie from the bowels of hell, and it is satan's final verdict not ours and most certainly not God's! God promises that NOTHING and He means absolutely NOTHING can separate us from His love! (Romans 8:39-39) A loving father loves and disciplines his children, so will God but it is not wrath coming upon us because Jesus already took our punishment for anything we could ever do past, present or future. (Proverbs 3:12)

As a baby learns to crawl, we learn to eventually soar with Holy Spirit however the beginning stages of our Christian walk can be a slippery slope at times, but rest assured The Lord always catches us and lifts us up. Although there was so much Glory in the beginning of my walk with Jesus, I was still very wounded and continued to allow the cycles of abuse, leading to one separation after another until finally a divorce. I was very co-dependent, and my ex-husband was a narcissist who needed healing in his heart and to allow The Love of Jesus to heal and bring forth his identity but sadly during our marriage this did not transpire. I threw myself into ministry full force and while a broken vessel myself, I moved in The Love of Jesus yet continued striving and striving because somewhere in my soul, I still felt I had to perform to earn God's love because of my past rejections and trauma.

I remember such a powerful encounter with The Lord the winter of 2015 when The Voice of God spoke to me so clearly that He was my True Father, and my parents were just earthen vessels. He spoke into my heart that Jesus redeems the "orphan spirit" and there was such a healing that took place in my heart that forever marked me with love and a sense of identity.

An orphan functioning in ministry is a dangerous thing because while The Anointing is flowing, the wounds are still "bleeding" and there sadly are many orphans in the church and many are operating in gifting yet "hemorrhaging" deep open wounds! I know because I was one of them and in fact it is sadly prevalent throughout the body of Christ.

Church hurts will come and go, when you still have wounding, this will create spiritual scar tissue that only the loving and tender finger of The Lord can remove and heal! No amount of deliverance or inner healing can penetrate deep enough if you still believe even a fraction of the lies of satan regarding your identity! God wants us to let Him Father us and believe every word He has spoken over us in The Word and personally to us.

Once we fully embrace this, the journey gets much smoother, and we can walk out upon the waters of purpose and ride the waves of destiny with Jesus. When God spoke: *Jeremiah 29:11 "For I know The Plans I have for you declares The Lord, plans for peace and not evil, to give you a future and a hope"* He meant *exactly* this literally. He has The Master Plan, He holds The Blueprints in His Hand, He has called you by name and you are His! (Reference Isaiah 43) No matter what has been done to you, who threw you away like a piece of discarded clothing, no matter who used and abused you... He still lovingly resounds this promise over your life, and you can take that to the bank treasured child of God.

It is never ever too late. He wants you to partner with His Heart and say, "Yes!" He will do the rest and turn your life into a story of

Glory, a story of Restoration, a story of hope and healing... watch and see!

During these glorious and tender moments in The Glory of His Presence during our Secret Place time, He reveals His Heart and plans for our lives as though opening a scroll from His Heart and He will confirm His Word in many ways such as a scripture, a song, nature, a friend, or through a Man or Woman of God and sometimes during a worship service.

When God gave me my "marching orders" to write this book, I never saw myself as an author, I had always been a song and poetry writer and blogging was about the extent of it; however He clearly spoke to me during a time of corporate worship that I would write this book called **Hijacked Identity** and He would bring healing and comfort to those who read this book as well as a fresh wind of His love and a whisper of destiny into hearts.

The Glory opens realms and portals of Heaven and the scrolls of our lives, our books He wrote with His very finger!

What holds you back? For me it was insecurity and fear of failure, but He is persistent to remind us it is His works we are doing with Him... *not by might, not by power...only by His Spirit.*
(Zechariah 4:6)

No matter what He has called you to do from being a parent, a teacher, a cashier, a business person in the marketplace, a Preacher, an Evangelist, part of The Fivefold Ministry, a singer, a musician, a waiter, a barista, I could go on and on but no matter how small you might feel in the moment... remember you were created for Glory in His Image to be a gift to this world and bring hope, love and comfort. Dare to dream again with Jesus, dare to dust off those dreams you set on the shelf or those promises you thought were shattered for you were truly created for such a time of this and there is Glory arising in the midst.

"For if you remain silent at this time, relief and deliverance will arise for the Jews from another place and you and your father's house

will perish. And who knows whether you have not attained royalty for such a time as this?"
Esther 4:14 NASB1995

"I want them back, every last one who bears my name, every man, woman, and child Whom I created for my glory, yes, personally formed and made each one."
Isaiah 43:7 MSG

For we are His workmanship [His own master work, a work of art], created in Christ Jesus [reborn from above—spiritually transformed, renewed, ready to be used] for good works, which God prepared [for us] beforehand [taking paths which He set], so that we would walk in them [living the good life which He prearranged and made ready for us]. Ephesians 2:10 AMP

Prayer: Lord, I cry out to You ..." Here I am Lord send me! Father, for every squandered moment, every moment of delay and procrastination, for every time I ran and hid or listened to the wrong voice telling me who I am and what I am called to do, I repent and renounce any false beliefs and lies and I receive Your tender mercy and love which are new every morning. Father, I believe everything that is written in my book that You hold as a scroll in Your Heart. I declare I will accomplish all these wonderful things with You leading and guiding me. Lord, I want to leave nothing unfulfilled that You have asked for me to do, so I ask for a fresh fire right now, a fresh anointing in The Name of Jesus. Breathe on me Lord, blow away the spiritual "dust" and "cobwebs." I have my spiritual running shoes on now and I am ready to run with Fire! Jesus be Glorified in my life become what You dreamed for me so that together we can change this world and bring many sons and daughters out of darkness and into Your Marvelous Light in Jesus Glorious Name – Amen and Amen!

Activation: Write down the vision that The Lord gave you and place it on your bathroom mirror or in a place you will see it frequently. Make it fun, be creative, see yourself in your calling and declare it boldly every day... even right this moment! This is Biblical and you can find the scripture in Habakkuk 2:2.

Doing this will keep you motivated and focused so you can truly "run with it."

You have all of Heaven rooting for you and cheering you on! Run – Run – Run with Fire for The Glory of The Lord!

We will all cross the finish line if we keep our eyes on The Prize, King Jesus!

Do you feel His delight in you right now? He is so very pleased with you and is rejoicing in His Good – Glorious plans for your life! They are tangible right now to you by simply believing that you were strategically and lovingly planned and placed upon this earth to have a unique blueprint to reach specific people groups. Jesus has given you supernatural "keys" that will unlock hearts of stone and cause chains to shatter as you realize "The Kingdom of Heaven is within you" because you are filled with The Holy Spirit and Fire of God.

As the Disciples walked with Jesus and turned the world upside down, we are commissioned and anointed to do the very same thing! There is so much hurt and hopelessness in the world and you are called to bring liberty to the captive as Jesus did! (Isaiah 61)

Chapter Ten

The Unraveling

When Jesus called Lazarus back to life, there
was an unraveling in the natural realm of the
grave clothes and Jesus gave the command
"Loose him and let him go!" some versions say,
"unwrap him and release him!" (John 11:44)
This is both literally and spiritually as the spirit
of death and infirmity had bound him
spiritually, as the grave clothes bound
him physically!

This likewise is true for many who have been
bound in satan's spider web of lies! The lies of
the enemy will have you believing you have
gone too far, and God is done with you, you are
not smart enough, not pretty enough, not fast
enough, not qualified and the sticky – ugly
tangled web wraps around and around until
you literally feel the effects in your physical
body as well.

Often a parent, grandparent, aunt, uncle, sibling, teacher, friend, husband, wife, even someone in ministry can speak carelessly and cause deep-deep wounding because the enemy used their tongue often without them even realizing it, to fire a dart of destruction. Sometimes, we ourselves have spoken so unkindly over our own lives and repeated thoughts that the enemy has bombarded us with, and this leads to further identity loss which is the goal of satan to hijack our God breathed identity which is only found in Jesus!

I can remember even in ministry people saying such cruel words that in essence were "word curses" and because I was not rooted and grounded in Love, I took the bait and believed this was God's Heart for me, which was in fact a purposeful weapon of destruction sent forth from the enemy's camp to entangle me deeper and deeper in this web! When this cycle begins it is very subtle; but over time it wraps and wraps tightly around a person until the very essence of God's DNA that is lovingly weaved into every fiber of your being, becomes choked out like weeds coming into a beautiful garden that God created just for you. The more tightly wrapped in this web will cause your vision and the fertile soil in your heart to become blinded, unable to neither see nor receive properly; it will be like a warped kaleidoscope of deception!

A person who is struggling to get out of this web, will often read The Word and believe but deep down a false root system will whisper more accusations and lies such as "yes maybe for them, but not for you, you have done too many things wrong" and the barrage of these "spiritual vultures" will cause hope deferred and a sense of foreboding which becomes the "Spiritual gravestone" blocking the entrance into the lush, exquisite garden of destiny that God has for you.

God being The Loving, Kind Father that He is stops at nothing to illuminate the truth, no matter what it takes. His pursuit is lavishly relentless and fierce, and He will give you dreams, visions, send messengers who are sensitive to His Heart and Spirit! Our Father will not be mocked, for the very reason He sent Jesus and the finished work of The Cross. His Heart's cry has always been to gather His

children the way a mother hen gathers her
chicks under her wings!
(Matthew 23:37)

I was so bound up and entangled that even
when God would speak something so
profoundly tender and beautiful to me, the
rejection that I lived in so long would
figuratively put a shield up because I did not
know how to receive or perceive love. I was
not perfected in Perfect Love. I would receive
glorious prophetic dreams and when delay
sang her song over me, I would allow the song
of delay to be louder than the "Songs of Love
and Deliverance" that my Father was singing
so sweetly to me. The voice of pain and shame,
regret and fear were drowning out the
"Cadences of Heaven" because my identity had
been hijacked even from my mother's womb.

This is so insidious because Scripture clearly
declares in:
*Jeremiah 1:5 "Before I formed you in the
womb, I knew you; Before you were born,
I sanctified you;
I ordained you a prophet to the nations."
NKJV*

We were sanctified and set apart, holy unto the Lord yet the enemy of our soul targets a future generation even before fully developed and formed in the womb.

This can look like thoughts of abortion or adoption, stress upon the mother when the baby in her womb, negative words spoken over the unborn child, a parent only wanting a boy or girl, gender confusion due to a parent dressing a boy like a girl and a girl like a boy. The evil one sows seeds of lies such as "I was born this way" or "I would have been better off not born" the way he sows these lies is through agreement of the word and the word being watered with poison through a parent, grandparent, ourselves or any other person speaking this out and us accepting it as factual.

God spoke loud and clear when scripture states "He made them male and female" we can see this from Genesis 1:27 – all the way through the New Testament where Jesus reiterated this subject matter.

"But from the beginning of the creation, God 'made them male and female. For this reason, a man shall leave his father and mother and be joined to his wife, and the two shall become one flesh'; so, then they are no longer two, but one flesh."
Mark 10:6-8

Love and only Love from Father God's heart and Truth can break the cycles and shackles of these lies but never condemning words, for sin is sin and we all have fallen short of The Glory of God! There are many powerful men and woman of God who at one time were bound by lies and lived a homosexual lifestyle until Jesus revealed Himself Gloriously and His kiss of Love changed the course of their lives to bring many into The Family. Often a child experiences trauma in the womb and enters the world feeling grief at their arrival as opposed to light and love. The chaos of the parent's words and emotions particularly the mother carrying the child has an effect on the child to more of a deep degree than many realize.

Jesus has always been and always will be The Lover of our Souls and Healer of our Hearts and He is ready and willing to heal these soul wounds and reveal how much rejoicing went on in Heaven the very day you made your "grand entrance" into this world! Your scrolls were sealed, and The Lord wants to unroll them because you have a very unique and special assignment and it is time to accept how very precious and dearly loved you are and that your birth, no matter if planned or unplanned; it **WAS** planned by Father God!

So, you may be wondering "how do I get unraveled?" You may have bought every self-help book, prayed, fasted, quoted Scripture, sought deliverance (which I am all for these wonderful tools and have used every one of these tools myself!) Yet, until you are fully persuaded and know like you know, deep inside who you are and believe The Truth of what God says about YOU, it will just be another trip around the mountain without ever getting to your destination. Believe me, I had so many cycles around the mountain also, and I was "battle weary"!

God will never, and I mean never – ever stop pursuing you. He will get His Heart and point through no matter how long you have been going around and around! Remember when Jesus got word that Lazarus was gravely ill, He delayed His trip 2 additional days? (John 11:3-6) His love was deep, and He even wept but He was focused on the *BIGGER Picture,* The Glory of God was to be revealed and the "scroll of Lazarus Life" (his book in Heaven) to be fulfilled. No Stone blocking any entrance of Glory whether physical, spiritual or emotional can stop The Love and Steadfastness of God, our Amazing – Loving Father! What is the stone that has gotten in your way, keeping you bound and locked in "the grave of lies"?

For me, I was deeply wounded even from birth and had years of rejection, abandonment, abuse and a "bad crop" of lies that had been watered with satan's poison. I had tried everything but as The Woman with the issue of blood, I knew if I could only touch the very

hem of Jesus' Garment, I would be made
whole! (Luke 8:43-48)

My unraveling was one of such a Beautiful
Father who did *EVERYTHING* to reach me and
I seriously mean *EVERYTHING!* From
dreams, visions, prophecy and repeating
lovingly and so patiently His plans for me
through many vessels He sent to me until I
finally had my aha moment!

I was a "late bloomer" spiritually so to speak
however once the light comes on brightly, all
the darkness and lies begin to vanish and
realization sets in that there is a war going on
in the realm of the spirit to hijack your identity
and bring destruction. Learning to trust and
believe these amazing words and plans for me
was a process yet the fruit that comes forth
once the weeds of deception and lies are
uprooted and the beautiful garden springs
forth, making the process comparable to a
woman giving birth. I can remember the
details and the hurt, yet no longer is there pain.
I know that I was sent forth with a plan and
purpose for such a time as this and I can say
boldly that "what the enemy has meant to

harm me, God has turned to bring hope, healing and deliverance for His Glory!" When Joseph came into his destiny and purpose and was reconciled with his brothers, he was *radiant with revelation* and my friend... that is your story too! (Genesis 45)

Then Joseph said to his brothers, "I am Joseph! Is my father still alive?" But his brothers were speechless, for they were stunned and dismayed by [the fact that they were in] Joseph's presence.
And Joseph said to his brothers, "Please come closer to me." And they approached him. And he said, "I am Joseph your brother, whom you sold into Egypt. Now do not be distressed or angry with yourselves because you sold me here, for God sent me ahead of you to save life and preserve our family."
Genesis 45:3-5 AMP

Therefore, his sisters sent unto him, saying, Lord, behold, he whom thou lovest is sick. When Jesus heard that, he said, this sickness is not unto death, but for the glory of God, that

the Son of God might be glorified thereby.
Now Jesus loved Martha, and her sister, and
Lazarus. When he had heard therefore that he
was sick, he abode two days still in the same
place where he was.
John 11:3-6 NKJV

Prayer: Father, I desire to be fully unraveled in Jesus Name. I do not want to delay not even another day of fulfilling what You have written in my books. I want the scroll of my life to unfold and to leave the pain and the past behind. Thank You Father for stopping at absolutely nothing to roll away any stone hindering me from walking in my calling. Lord, my declaration is from this day forward "I am radiant with revelation!" in Jesus Mighty Name – Amen!

Activation: Imagine Jesus unraveling you from all the lies, the sticky residue of the web of deception. See Him, swirling you around as He calls you forth into your destiny. Hear His voice as He tells you "Child of destiny, you are a treasure to Me, rise and shine in My Glory and Love!" *Feel* yourself being "undone", "unraveled", and *FREE* to answer the call of The Bridegroom!

The one I love calls to me: Arise, my dearest. Hurry, my darling. Come away with me! I have come as you have asked to draw you to my heart and lead you out. For now, is the time, my beautiful one.
Song of Songs 2:10 TPT

Being unraveled and undone looks glorious on you! Jesus wants to walk with you through the "garden of your heart", He has been pulling up the weeds and He is handing you a beautiful bouquet of *"flowers of promise"* that have bloomed in His love!
He is The Master Gardner and loves to dance with you in the "Garden of His Love"!

Chapter Eleven

Radiant with Revelation

You have come a long way my friend, and my prayer for you is that you have had or will very soon experience a tangible encounter with The Father's Heart and Love for you and are ready to be "Radiant with Revelation."

You have carried the "heavy backpack" of trauma, pain, rejection, abandonment, and lies for far too long and Jesus is thrilled to take it in exchange for His beautiful – easy and light yoke! That looks something like, allowing Him to define you and unwind you, laying your cares and burdens down even if you have tried time and time again. Jesus is always praying and making intercession for us and when The Holy Spirit was sent to us, we have the entire Kingdom of God within us!

Holy Spirit wants you to rest upon His chest just like John the Beloved did with Jesus. (John 13:23) We can experience this in The Spirit and He will reveal secrets and strategies to us! What a beautiful *promise ring* The Lord placed within us by sending The Third Person of The Trinity to us. The gift of this Amazing Love is that when Jesus said, "It is better I should go away" (John 16:17) did we really understand, the beauty that was bestowed to us? Jesus desires all His beloved ones to be able to walk and talk with Him just as He and the disciples had such a precious deep union.

Jesus could only be in one place at one time during His time on earth in human form, yet Holy Spirit is with each one of us and wants to walk with you every day.

Holy Spirit will take you through "School of The Spirit" if you yield to Him being your Rabbi (Teacher) and just as Jesus proclaimed over Simon, *"You are Peter and upon this rock I will build My Church and the gates of Hell shall not prevail against it!"* (Matthew 16:18) Holy Spirit will speak strength and encouragement and declare destiny over you.

What have you dreamed that was so vibrant that you woke up feeling The Anointing with such inspiration? What have you heard Holy Spirit reveal to you? No matter the opposition, in the battle one thing is certain... Heaven declared it, your scrolls are alive with the very Breath of God and only we have the option to forfeit it and not let it come forth to full term!

As we look at the life of David when he was a young shepherd boy, after Samuel poured the Horn of Oil upon him *(1 Samuel 16:13)*, he knew his destiny, The Holy Spirit remained with him but what happened right after his first glorious victory with Goliath?
(1 Samuel 17)

Just one chapter over and we see how warfare and betrayal began following David's victory, because satan attempts to mock God and His people and will try to convince you that you cannot do it, and in one way he is right... *we cannot do it without Holy Spirit!*

You are a mighty warrior in God's Kingdom and your assignment is ordained by God, He has provided you Holy Armor (Ephesians 6) and breathed His Spirit into you. You are equipped and no matter how loud satan tries to roar, The Mighty Lion of The Tribe of Judah, our King Jesus, Roars LOUDER and with *The* ONLY TRUE AUTHORITY! Settle for nothing less then what God has revealed to you and see it! No matter what appears to be limited, our God is limitless, and it is never-ever too late!

If you research through The Bible many of our Patriots started their journey at latter points in their lives. Time was only created for us; God is outside of time and even right now let's say a loud and joyous **Hallelujah** for that truth!

A woman with child is often said to be "radiant", "glowing", we are pregnant with destiny and purpose and are "Radiant with Revelation"! When a couple finds out they are expecting a baby, there is preparation and planning, an expectancy to be ready to deliver this baby!

When Hadassah was brought to the palace to become Queen Esther, she went through a season of preparation with beauty treatments with eager expectation to be Queen. You are receiving your time of preparation by soaking in The Anointing of The Holy Spirit, resting in the Beauty of The Lord and listening to the instructions of The Holy Spirit as you read The Word and meditate!

In my own personal journey, I have had to encourage myself in The Lord the way the Psalmist David did. It was not always easy and God never promised us easy but did secure our Victory through the finished work of The Cross and our books in Heaven that He personally wrote and blessed!

Being "Radiant with Revelation", I liken this to Mary when The Angel Gabriel came to her and told her she would conceive a child from The Holy Spirit. As profoundly impossible as it seemed for a young virgin to conceive a child, let alone the very Son of God, Mary received "The Seed" of The Rhema Word released by The Angel of The Lord and a divine radiance overtook her with great joy, even before the Holy Encounter with The Holy Spirit to bring forth the manifestation! (Luke 1:26-38) Mary, as we know, did not exactly have a "cake walk" following this powerful encounter! In fact, the warfare was so intense upon her life that she had to hold her head high even as accusations and fingers pointed at her negatively. That precious seed within her heart was already deeply rooted and she knew God highly favored her and hand selected her! Mary's identity was now shifted to the mother of our Beloved Lord and Savior which carried her through the trials facing her.

Enduring in hard seasons is not easy, and perhaps you have had a long-long season of waiting, enduring and "drought".

There is so much we can learn from those who went before us believing, trusting, never giving up and persevering.
(Hebrews 11 The Faith Chapter)

Let me encourage you by The Spirit that nothing has been wasted, not one precious tear. You will see a harvest of joy as you wait for the "water of your destiny" to break...and once you see the tangible birth of the long-awaited promise, there will be no stopping you! You are Glowing and so very Radiant with Revelation that you will be like a deep well, ready to bring "The Water of The Word" to many thirsty and weary souls! You will shift atmospheres because you have been through the fire, the storms, the afflictions and never have quit!

Once I realized how crystal clearly God was speaking to me, so patiently time and time again to my destiny and purpose, it was as though a veil was lifted and scales fell off my eyes! I saw that there was a force behind all the pain, rejection, confusion and I was ready to take God at His Word even though there were many tears and setbacks. Satan will come back at "a more opportune" time to try to see if we will take his bait again or buckle to his accusations against The Living God and His plans for your life. Remaining focused on Jesus and partnering with Heaven in agreement to God's plan and purpose for your life giving you strength for the journey.

We all were placed here as a gift from God to reach someone, no matter the assignment. You have already been anointed with oil from The Holy Spirit and Jesus gave the great commission to go forth!

To see The Kingdom filled with precious souls is a "multivitamin" to your spirit! God will give you the endurance and tenacity to keep propelling forward under The Wind of His Spirit, so keep getting up warrior; it is your time to shine! It is your time to give birth to your promise, the water is about to break as you PUSHHHH!

"Shall I bring to the moment of birth and not give delivery?" says the Lord.
"Or shall I who gives delivery shut the womb?" says your God.
Isaiah 66:9 AMP

But Mary kept all these sayings, pondering them in her heart.
Luke 2:19 ASV

Prayer: Father, I thank You for the "seed of promise" You have impregnated me with. I trust You to bring forth the delivery of these precious promises that will bring great Glory to

Your Holy Name. I know that You will give me the strength to PUSH when the "water of my destiny" breaks and I will give birth to **all** that You have written in my scrolls with Your very Finger in Jesus Mighty and Victorious Name – Amen and Amen!
Hallelujah!!!

Decree: *"I decree and declare in The Authority and Power of The Word, that I shall not miscarry or abort my destiny! I will carry this precious seed that is growing in me to full term and when "my water of destiny breaks" I will PUSHHHHHHH knowing that I have made myself ready by faith, seeing the promise as Abraham and Sarah did in Jesus Glorious and Victorious Name – Amen!"*

Chapter Twelve

Getting into The Birthing Position

*A*s a woman with child takes prenatal vitamins to keep her and the baby strong and healthy during her pregnancy, pondering the promises in your heart as Mary did, seeing it, meditating on The Word and the Promises God gave you and journaling your promises and words received is a supernatural "prenatal vitamin"! Often as the pregnancy progresses a woman may feel tired from carrying the child for 9 months. We must not grow weary as we carry our promise to full term. Yes, we will have days where we feel we are far from the delivery, and yes we will have days that we have to pick up our journals and read every promise God personally gave us and declare *"It is settled, God said it and I believe it!"*

You might even wonder, *"Lord, You gave me the assignment and I am the least qualified"*! I have said that so many times particularly when He gave me the assignment of this book, but my friend... *"God does not call the qualified, He qualifies the called!"* God will take the very area you struggle in and your biggest battles and turn those into flowing streams of healing and hope to share with others. We were made for Victory and we were designed to conquer here on this earth in the apostolic anointing Jesus commissioned each one of us with when He said we would do even greater things! (John 14:12)

So, no matter how dark and seemingly dirty your past was or even whatever battle you are facing right now, you can rest assured that The Very God of The Universe, Your Father was not taken aback by or shaken, for He is UNSHAKABLE! He doesn't fall off of His Throne gasping in shock and horror, but in fact He loves and adores you and rejoices over you with triumphant singing. (Zephaniah 3:17)

The hardest battle you will ever have to fight is the battle that goes on in your mind, but our battle cry is love because we are rooted and grounded in His Perfect Love! When I first realized the scheme of satan was to hijack my identity and thwart my destiny, I did have some breaking up of fallow ground to deal with as well as realizing that although I may feel "shipwrecked" at times, I have an "Oasis in The Lord" always! The Apostle Paul was shipwrecked on 3 different occasions, yet he was able to stand unmovable-unshakeable because he heard God's voice and instruction clearly which empowered him to encourage others who were about to drown in despair! (Acts 27:25)

Running with your eyes looking forward is a key to victory, if we are always looking back, we will stumble. I stumbled many – many times but I kept getting back up.

The Holy Spirit will encourage you to stand and keep going, He will spur you on and whisper little "love notes" from The Father to keep you focused and the Fire burning within you. Jesus gave us a brand-new life in Him, we are a new creation (2 Corinthians 5:17) and while the enemy would love to take the "dust of our past" and reconstruct walls and barriers, we are created to leave the dust behind us and

with God we are ABLE to leap over walls!
(Psalm 18:29)

The size of your giant is only a puny ant to
God, and we can plow forth by His Spirit! In
my own ministry I have had my voice attacked,
my character, my reputation, my finances, my
health and the accusations of the enemy
sneering and spewing venom to try to trap me
in his snare of lies.

Think about it... Jesus Himself was led into the
wilderness *by The Spirit* to be tempted by the
devil immediately following His baptism yet
because He was also baptized in The Fathers
Perfect Love; He was able to withstand the
temptation. Jesus was here on earth, perfectly
God, and perfectly man to show us we can do
ALL Things through Him, for He is our
strength! (Philippians 4:13)

Jesus was immersed in His Father's Love and
the resounding Voice *"This is My Beloved Son
in Whom I AM well pleased!"* (Matthew 3:17)
kept Him focused on His destiny and His
Fathers Voice became His only reality, no
matter the jeers and sneers of the evil one

spewing "if you are the Son of God..." one accusation upon another! Can you imagine the very audacity of satan to try to hijack even Jesus' Identity?

It is so hard to even fathom how satan thought he could be like God (Isaiah 14:14) and then to believe he could take Jesus off course! That is why he fell like lightening and Jesus had already witnessed that before He was sent on His earthly assignment! (Luke 10:18) The enemy knows if he can get into your head and convince you of his lie, that it will delay you and could cause you to miscarry or abort your assignment! The Grace and Love of God will always chase us down because we win... Jesus is our Victorious Warrior and will NEVER stop this relentless pursuit of Love!

It is time to arise and shake off the dust; it is your season to boldly proclaim *"I WILL GIVE BIRTH TO MY DESTINY!!!"* You have been "pregnant with destiny" far too long and it is the season to get into "The Birthing Position" for your promises are "crowning" and the time is NOW! Creation has been groaning for the sons and daughters of God to arise and give birth to the fulfillment of destiny! (Romans 8:22) In fact Romans 8 is a beautiful - inspiring song of love over us that you can take to the bank, I encourage you to take the time to reflect and meditate upon this chapter as it is food to your very soul!

To posture yourself in "The Birthing Position" spiritually, is to merely become *"fully persuaded"* that you are who God says you are, and you will do all He said you will accomplish! You have Heaven as your cheerleading section and most importantly, your Holy Father's Blessing and Approval. A Father's Blessing is so beautiful and does so much in the realm of The Spirit, we see in the Old Testament so many examples of a Father blessing his children. Some of us have not had a father's blessing due to our many situations but rest assured... Your Abba Daddy God blesses you with the very same blessing He gave Jesus... *"You are My beloved child in whom I AM well pleased"* and He doesn't stop there... He will continue to bless the work of your hands as you seek Him daily!

Take steps each day towards the "vision", if it is to write... *begin,* simply by trusting the Holy Spirit to write with you and through you, if it is to Preach The Gospel, begin everywhere you go, in your own family, the grocery store, a podcast or your social media page, God will show you the path and never despise small-humble beginnings. Whatever the vision God gave you, the precious gifts and talents He placed inside you for this very season of time we are in, begin and begin again if need be. You were mantled to do the very things God has revealed to you, no one can take your mantle from you as long as there is breath inside you. It matters not if you are 19 or 119 years old, if you are alive, you have a divine purpose and reason because you are still on this earth, and *I decree right now that you will give birth to your destiny in Jesus Name!*

You were called, you were chosen and placed here to make a difference and God is lifting your head to show you The Glory before you. Your past does not define you nor do the lies that may have been spoken over you! God's Word shapes you and molds you into the precious -treasured child, His chosen vessel for the assignments He gave you.

Esau gave up his birthright (Genesis 25:29-34) and Jacob's name was changed to Israel (Genesis 32:22-32), so you can see how we can forfeit what God intends for our lives by allowing our flesh to override what God plans for us! It is time to take back all that the enemy has stolen; your birthright was purchased by The Blood of Jesus Christ and you are a joint heir with Jesus! (Romans 8:17)

You may be thinking, *"What if I already forfeited my birthright or what if my birthright was stolen from me?"* The Good News is... we are under the dispensation of Grace, thank You Jesus! We have been in some way, shape or form robbed of our birthright, our identity such as I was by my mother illegally changing my last name to hide my real father from me. Now in essence, she was trying to protect me in her own way but spiritually it did a lot, and I boldly took my "birthright back" following my divorce and when I started believing God no matter what I saw, felt or experienced. We are all still in process and are daily being molded into the beautiful image of King Jesus, it is a daily walk and a daily surrender! Aren't you glad His mercies are new every morning? I am so thankful for His Faithfulness! No matter what "trimester" you are in spiritually toward the arrival of your promises, you will give birth and once the arrival of your destiny occurs, you will allow the pain, the tears, the heartache to turn into ecstatic songs of praise! Child of promise, the "Kingdom Seed" is inside you and you, as Esther has come into the Kingdom for such a time as this!

Do you feel the labor pains of your promises? Are you ready to give birth? Allow Holy Spirit to assist you all the way into the "delivery room", the pushing; the contractions as they come faster and faster while the "baby of your promises crowns", you will push by faith what you once held in your heart, into a tangible – glorious destiny!

Get ready; get ready, get ready, it is time to give birth!

To this day we are aware of the universal agony and groaning of creation, as if it were in the contractions of labor for childbirth.
Romans 8:22 TPT

We are assured and know that [God being a partner in their labor] all things work together and are [fitting into a plan] for good to and for those who love God and are called according to [His] design and purpose.
Romans 8:22 AMPC

Prayer: Father, I believe you and I am ready to walk in all that You have pre-ordained for me. I accept and say YES to every assignment and destiny You have written in my Heavenly Scroll. I want to give birth to the destiny that You have before me, I am ready to give that final push to birth the miraculous and glorious future that You dreamed and planned for my life. For every word contrary to what You have spoken over me; whether it was by any authority figure such as a parent or leader, or any person, by any demonic force or even anything I spoke over myself... I ask You to forgive me now, and I renounce these words and render them null and void right now in Jesus Mighty Name! Father, I rejoice that I am carrying "Your Seed of Promise" and I go forth now in Your Blessing as a blessed and highly favored daughter/son of God. I posture my heart in "The Birthing Position" and I joyously await the moment of delivery in Jesus Name – Amen and Amen, Hallelujah!

Dream BIG Dreams child of Promise!

Activation: Name your "baby", knowing you are pregnant with "The Seed of Promise" it is time to prepare and give your "promise" a name. It may be simply writing down in your Bible, your journal or on a note card your destiny. Example: "Daughter of God", Son of God", "Author", "Evangelist", "Singer", "Preacher", "Mother", "Father", "Wife", "Husband", "Missionary", "Revivalist", "Doctor" "Nurse", "Business Owner" etc. but rest assured your "baby" has a last name called *"Breakthrough!"*

See yourself doing what has seemed only a dream and then walk into it, step by step, day by day!

Your "baby's" birth certificate is signed by God Almighty, Your Father who has already established it long before the very foundation of the earth! It is time to celebrate!

Prophetic Prayer from The Father's Heart

In closing, I would like to pray over you prophetically:

The Father would say to you, "You My treasured and beloved child are indeed The Apple of My eye, I dreamed of you, I desired you and I loved and knew you when you were only spirit. You are made for Glory child, and I bless you! I bless your destiny and the very work of your hands; I bless your life and never think for one moment I have been angry with you. I will continue to steer you along the right path for your life as you keep running to Me, especially when you "mess up", come to Me and we will fix it together! You were a dream come true in My heart when I formed your glorious substance of all the brilliantly vibrant colors of Eternity and wove you intricately inside your mother's womb!

I saw the hills, the valleys and the
mountaintops you would walk
through and I have established a beautiful –
broad place for your precious feet to walk
upon and occupy! My child, My very Own
beloved child, I have called you by name and
you are Mine, you have My Love, My
approval and My Blessing to go forth as My
Son Jesus did and turn this world upside
down to bring many more of My lost children
into My Kingdom of Love.
I AM rooting for you always!
With all My Love,
Abba"

I would love to hear from you, your
testimonies, your prayer request;
sandygoldmintz@gmail.com

106

Salvation Prayer

*I*f anyone has this book in their hands and does not know Jesus as their Lord and Savior and would like to know The Lover of your soul, simply repeat this prayer out loud:

"Heavenly Father, I admit I have sinned and I am deeply sorry and ask You to forgive me. Lord Jesus, I ask You to come and sit upon The Throne of my heart and be The Lord of my life, fill me with Your Holy Spirit and teach and walk with me each day, I ask this in Jesus Precious Name – Amen.

I want to be the first to say "Welcome to the family of God" if you prayed that prayer. Heaven is rejoicing and celebrating, and you are now a child of God! Hallelujah!

Jesus be Glorified in each precious beloved one's life as we embark on this journey together in union with You.

Touch each heart Lord and baptize them with Your Love fresh and new, so that they will hear You and see Your plans with The Spirit of Wisdom and Revelation seasoned in Your Perfect Love, In Jesus Glorious Name – Amen!

About the Author

*S*andy Goldmintz is a Psalmist, Prophetic Scribe and Author who has a fiery passionate zeal to see people free and saturated in The Love of The Father. As someone who struggled with identity, she has been given a mandate to help set the captives free from the lies and schemes of the enemy as an echo of God's Heart. Sandy's prayer is to help others take back their hijacked identities for The Glory of God.

Made in the USA
Columbia, SC
11 May 2024

35166370R00065